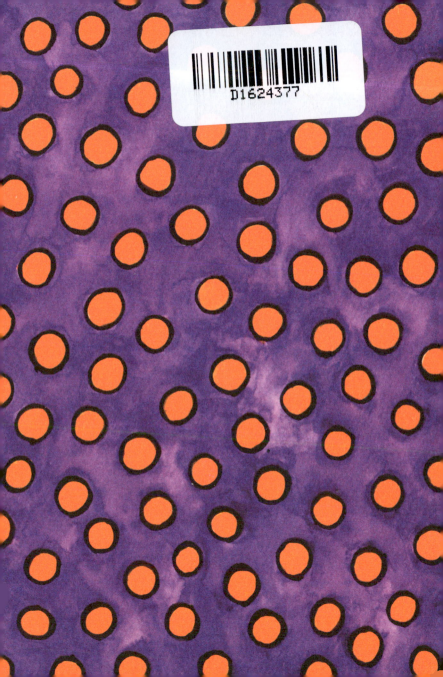

D1624377

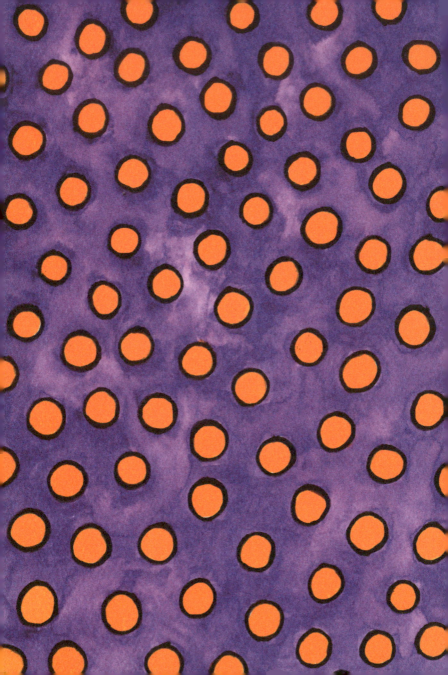

Cruisin' Through Life Is More Fun with Girlfriends

ISBN: 978-1-68088-349-7

◪ and Blue Mountain Press are registered in U.S. Patent and Trademark Office. Certain trademarks are used under license.

Printed in China.
First Printing: 2020

♺ This book is printed on recycled paper.

This book is printed on paper that has been specially produced to be acid free (neutral pH) and contains no groundwood or unbleached pulp. It conforms with the requirements of the American National Standards Institute, Inc., so as to ensure that this book will last and be enjoyed by future generations.

Blue Mountain Arts, Inc.
P.O. Box 4549, Boulder, Colorado 80306

Cruisin' Through Life Is More Fun with Girlfriends

Carolyn Stich

Blue Mountain Press™
Boulder, Colorado

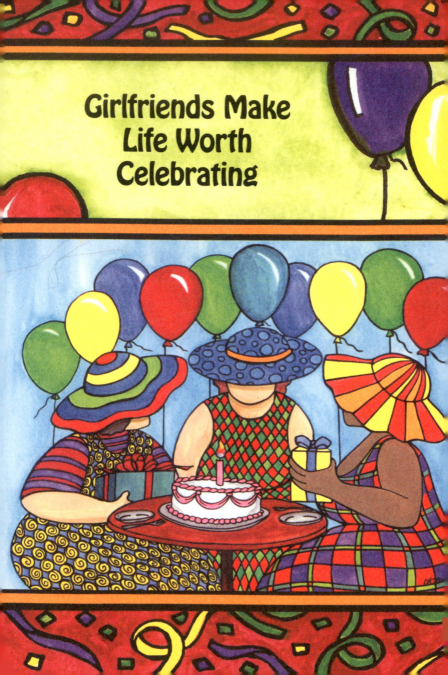

Girlfriends Make Life Worth Celebrating

The greatest gifts in life are girlfriends.
The relationships we share
can spark our imagination,
inspire our passions,
and drive us to be better.

Girlfriends like you
are worth a celebration...
every day.

Everything's Easier with Girlfriends and Ice Cream

Sometimes girlfriends may not even realize
we are making our best memories.
We are just setting our stresses aside
to share an easygoing moment
and solve all the world's problems
over a triple-scoop ice-cream cone.

Thank you for these unforgettable memories.

Girlfriends Keep Us Balanced and Help Us Find Our Inner Peace

Those moments with girlfriends
are vital to our inner peace
and overall sanity.

I am grateful for moments with you
where I can relax and be myself
and you have no expectations of me.

Coffee and Girlfriends
Create the Perfect Blend

On the good and not-so-good days,
girlfriends are there — mug in hand —
ready to listen.

I don't say it enough, but I appreciate
your ceaseless and sincere attention.
I hope to show that same sensibility
and kindness to you always.

Time with Girlfriends Is the Best Therapy

Every moment girlfriends spend together
seems to never be long enough.
We laugh louder, cry harder, and
dream bigger with one another.

You understand me, and my life is easier
with you by my side.

Girlfriends Are like Snowflakes, Every One Is Different... and Every One Is Beautiful

Girlfriends often have different
characteristics and different ideas.

My world is a better place because you
embrace and respect my ideas and opinions
as I accept and welcome yours,
even though there are differences.

The trust that girlfriends hold dearly
with one another is a treasure
beyond words.

How wonderful to know that
you are a friend and confidante
who will hold and cherish my secrets
as securely as your own.

Girlfriends Make the Cards We Have Been Dealt Easier to Play

Life is often compared to
a hand in a card game —
you make the best of what
you are dealt.

Your friendship has turned my cards
into a winning hand
full of fun and endless possibilities.

The Perfect Ingredients for Friendship

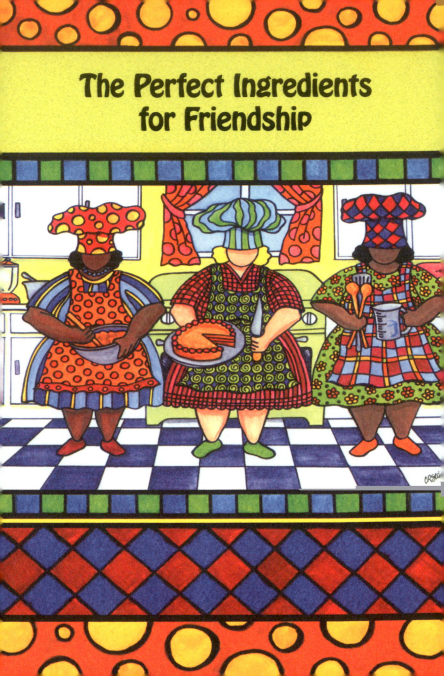

The perfect ingredients for friendship
are patience, kindness, humor,
bravery, honesty, joy, and love.

You are all of those wrapped up
in the most generous soul.

Sharing Adventures with Girlfriends Makes the Impossible Possible

Girlfriends escape the ordinary
and together create lifelong stories.
These stories are told over and over
with laughter and joy.

With you, my life is full
of happy adventures.

With Girlfriends, Life Is a Walk in the Park

There is nothing better than
a walk in the park with girlfriends.

The long conversations and even the quiet
times when we are just soaking in the scenery
add a certain kind of peace and tranquility
to life only found by spending time with you.

Girlfriends Are
Answered Prayers

The support and unconditional love
of girlfriends make everything
brighter and full of hope.

Through life's challenges,
I only have to look up
and see you are there —
an answered prayer.

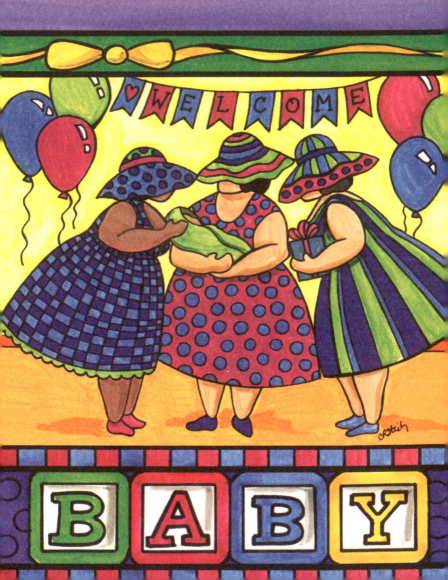

There are so many
beautiful experiences in life:
a young couple getting married,
a new puppy, a grand adventure,
a new home, a new baby.

All these special wonders are made greater
when I share them with you.

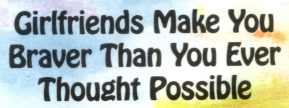

Girlfriends Make You Braver Than You Ever Thought Possible

The faith girlfriends have in one another
makes us courageous, strong,
and ready to face anything.

Whenever I am feeling unsure, I think of you.
Your unwavering belief in me makes me
braver than I ever thought possible.

Hugs from Girlfriends Help Us Through Hard Times

HOPE

When hard times hit
or difficult news is received,
a reassuring word or sincere hug
from our girlfriends is guaranteed.

Your presence during
trying times gives me comfort.

Time spent with girlfriends is
never wasted and always remembered.

When I'm with you,
my soul is in a contented place...
and when we are apart,
you are still in my heart.

Girlfriends Are the Core of All Things Sweet

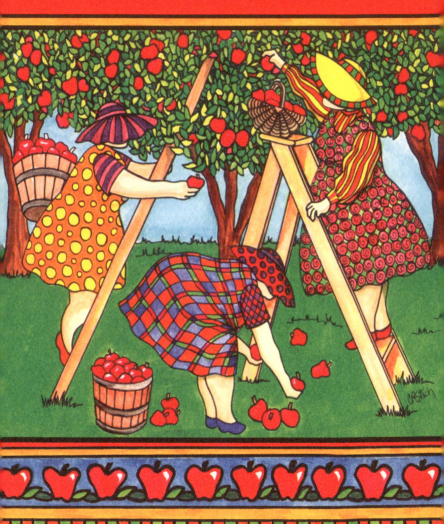

No matter how you slice it,
girlfriends add sweetness to life.

I am so very happy to
have gone out on a limb
and found the very best
girlfriend in you.

Cruisin' Through Life
Is More Fun with Girlfriends

Nothing is more uplifting
than a call from a girlfriend
with a simple request,
"Let's get away."

Thank you for sharing your
fun and fabulous spirit with me.

About the Author

Carolyn Stich has had the privilege of being an artist and gallery owner in downtown Holland, Michigan, for twelve years. She credits her success to the many wonderful people who have advised her along the way and given her great opportunities. Carolyn has illustrated ten children's books, along with countless commissioned pieces over the years. You can learn more about her and her art by visiting her website, www.carolynstich.com.

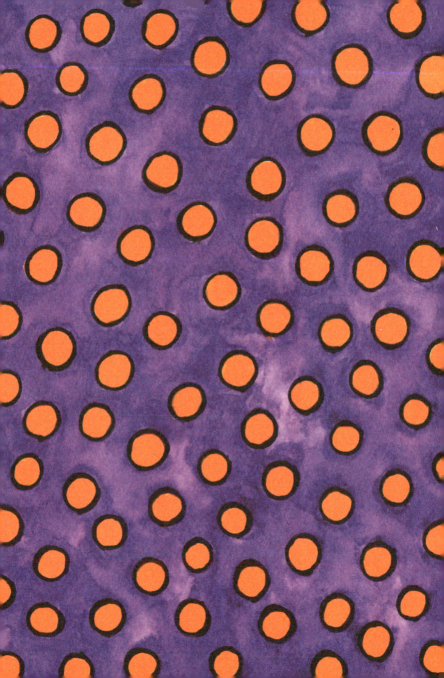

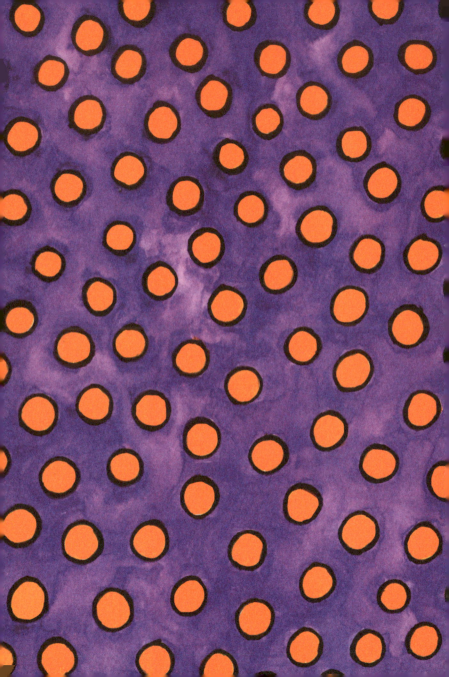